THE JAMES WEBB SPACE TELESCOPE

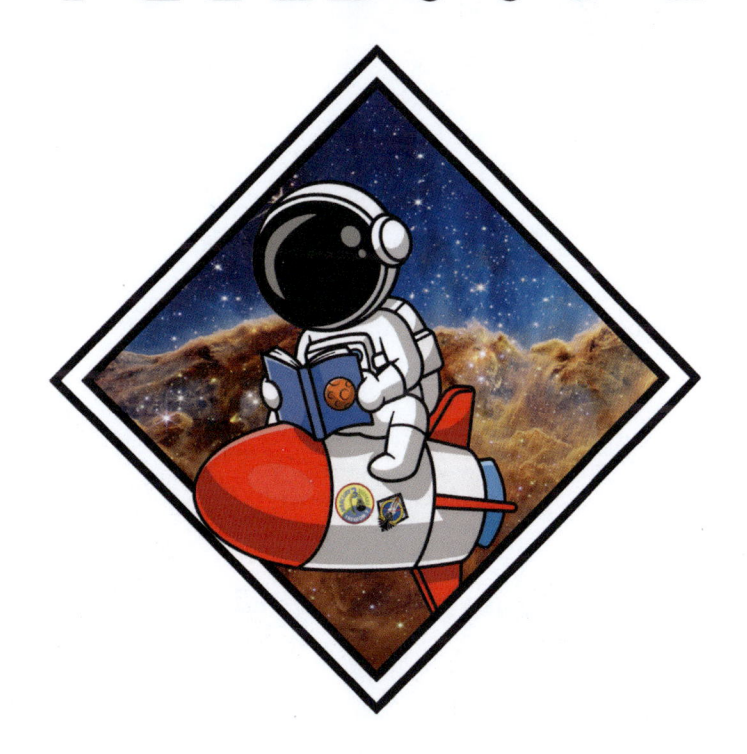

Copyright © 2022 Ulysses Press and its licensors. No part of this publication may be reproduced, stored in a retrieval system, or transmitted in any form or by any means without the prior written permission of the publisher, nor be otherwise circulated in any form of binding or cover other than that in which it is published and without a similar condition being imposed on the subsequent purchaser.

Published by:

ULYSSES PRESS
P.O. Box 3440
Berkeley, CA 94703
www.ulyssespress.com

Design and text by Keith Riegert

10 9 8 7 6 5 4 3 2 1

Image Credits: NASA and STScl. Shutterstock images ©: Jurik Peter, joshimerbin, Elena Schweitzer, Nolkin, D1min, muratart, ifH, Pike-28, Diana Hlevnjak, Catalyst Labs, BEST-BACKGROUND, Macrovector

Special thanks to NASA, STScl and all the amazing scientists and organizations that made this book possible.

NASA

The frontier is everywhere.

Hi future astronomers! I'm Astro and today I'd love to take you on a tour of the **James Webb Space Telescope**.

Together, we will get to see the first amazing pictures the telescope took of our universe!

Unlike satellites and other space telescopes, the **James Webb Space Telescope** doesn't orbit our planet—it orbits the sun.

To get to the telescope, we need to travel *1 million* miles away from Earth—that's four times arther away than the moon! It'll take us about one month to get there, so bring a suitcase!

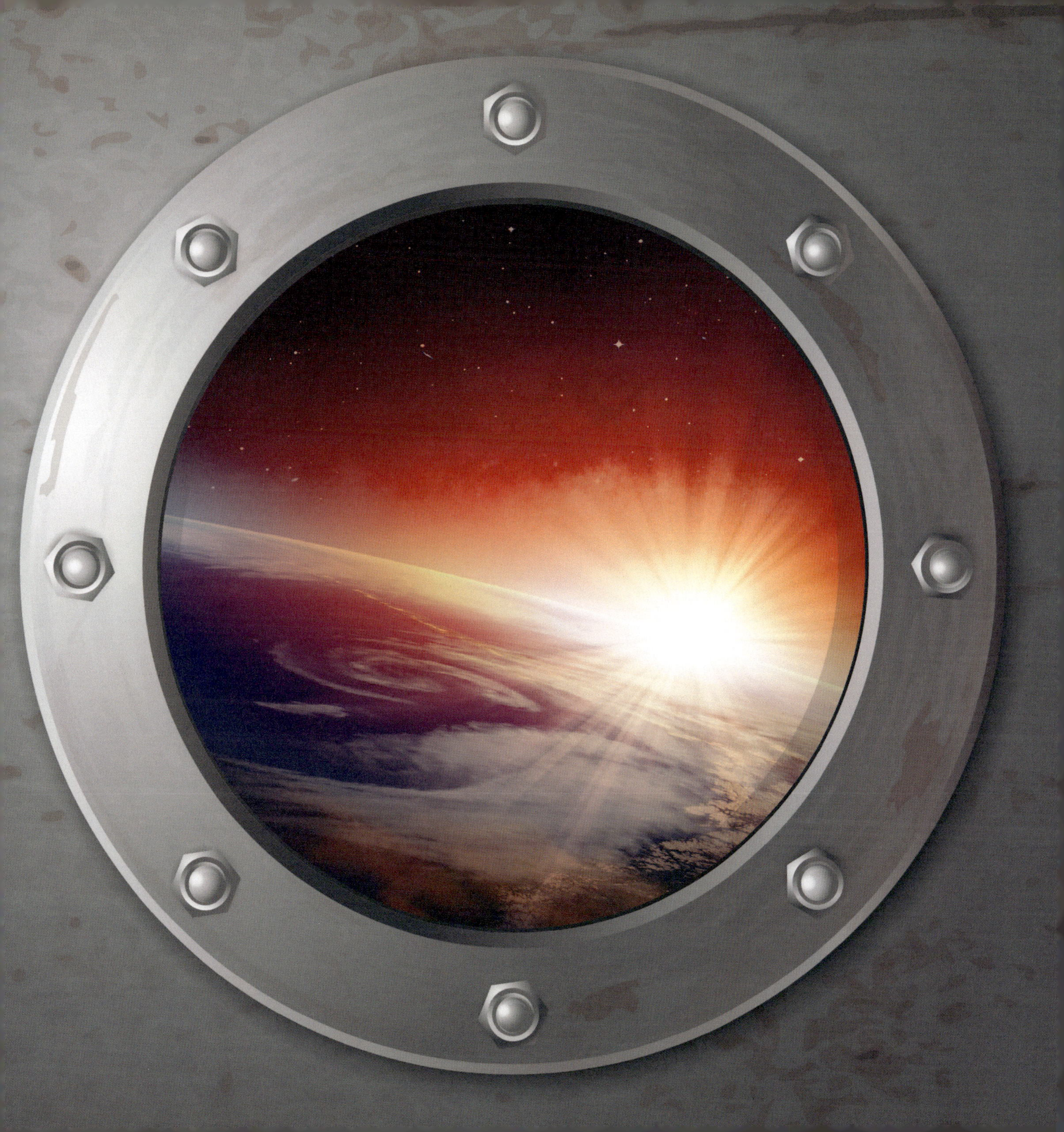

Made up of 18 hexagon-shaped mirrors, this is the most powerful space telescope ever launched.

The telescope is so strong it can see the very first stars and galaxies ever born in the universe—**13.6 BILLION** light years away.

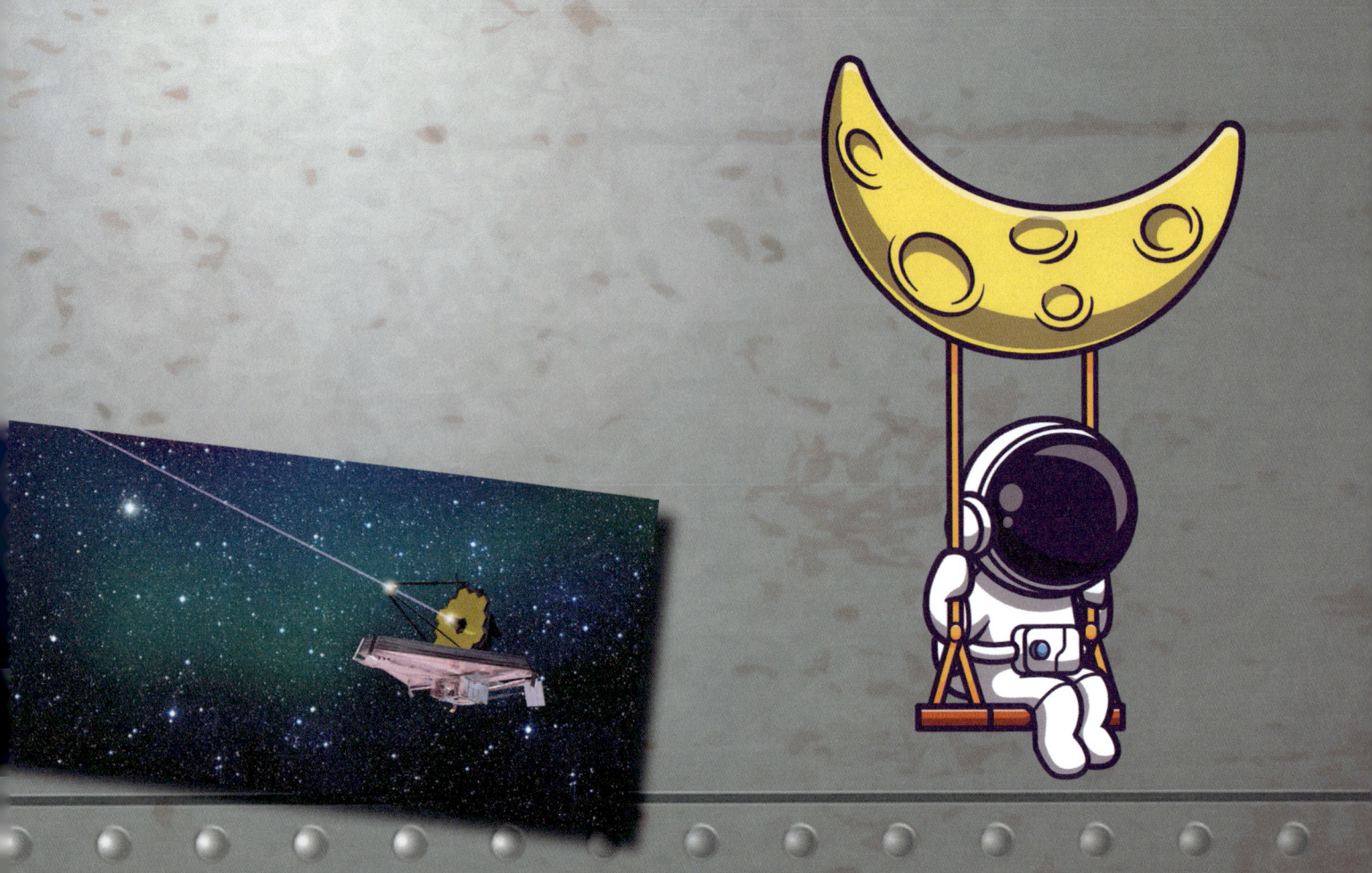

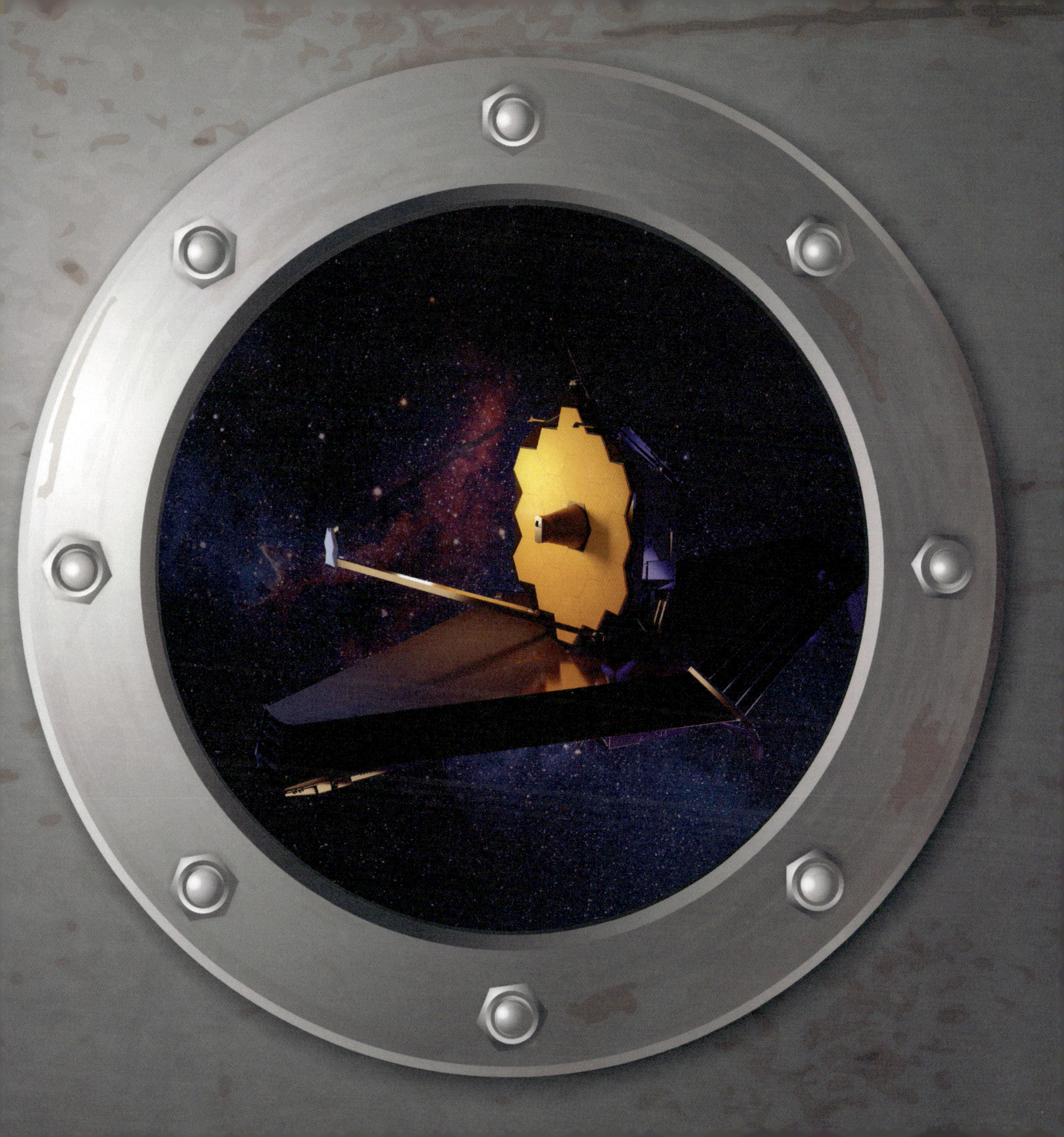

But before we look that far away, let's check in on one of our neighbors. The telescope snapped the most incredible picture ever taken of **Jupiter**, the largest planet in our solar system.

Can you find Jupiter's famous great spot?

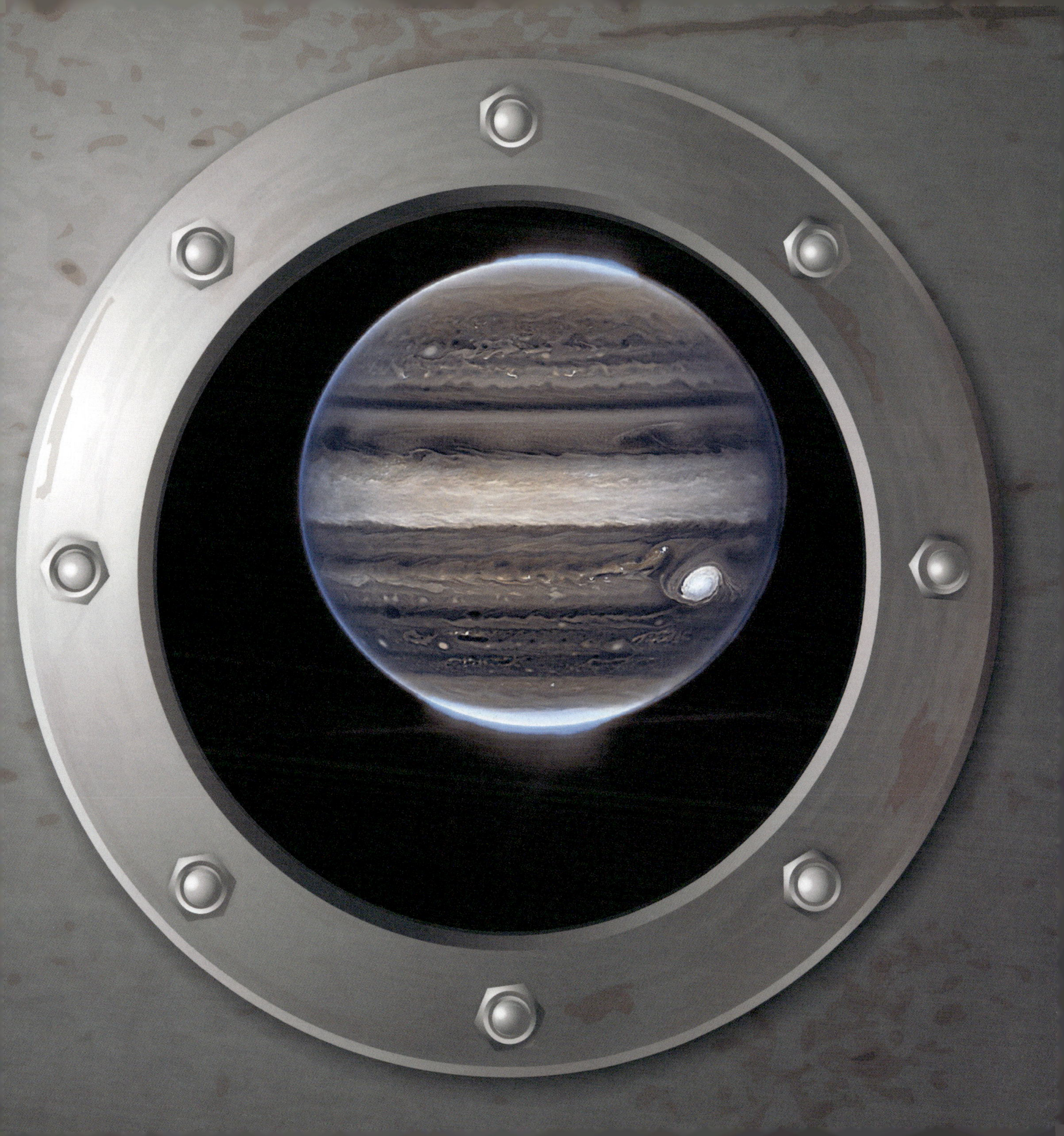

Have you ever seen an exploding star?

You have now! This is a picture of a star that once, very long ago, looked a lot like our own sun.

The **Southern Ring Nebula** is a white dwarf star that stopped burning fuel and now its gases make a big shell around where the star once was.

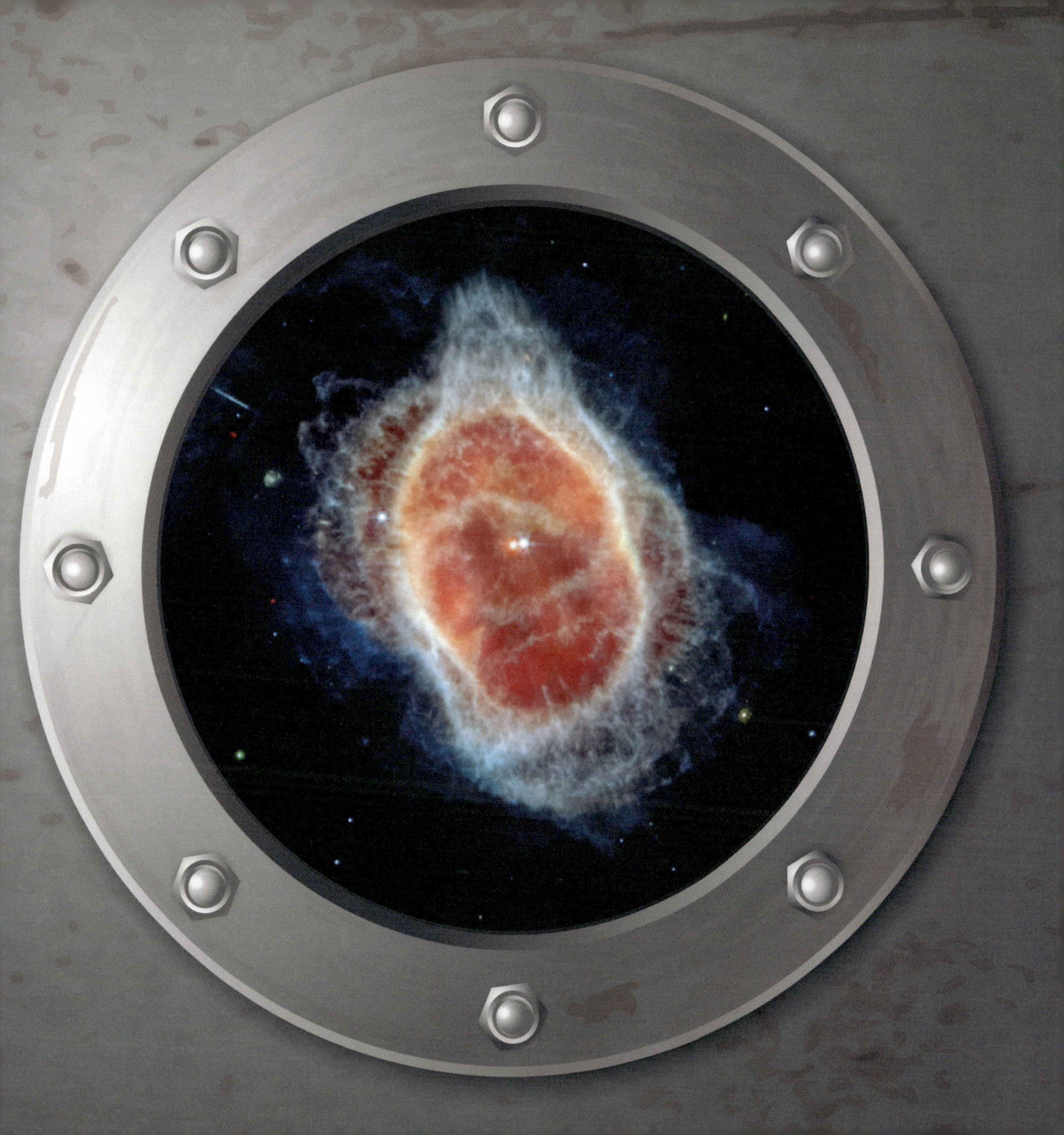

Unlike that exploding star, this is a picture of stars being *born*.

What looks like puffy clouds at night is actually called the **Cosmic Cliffs**. But these cliffs aren't rocky—they're made up of hot gases that are slowly forming into new stars.

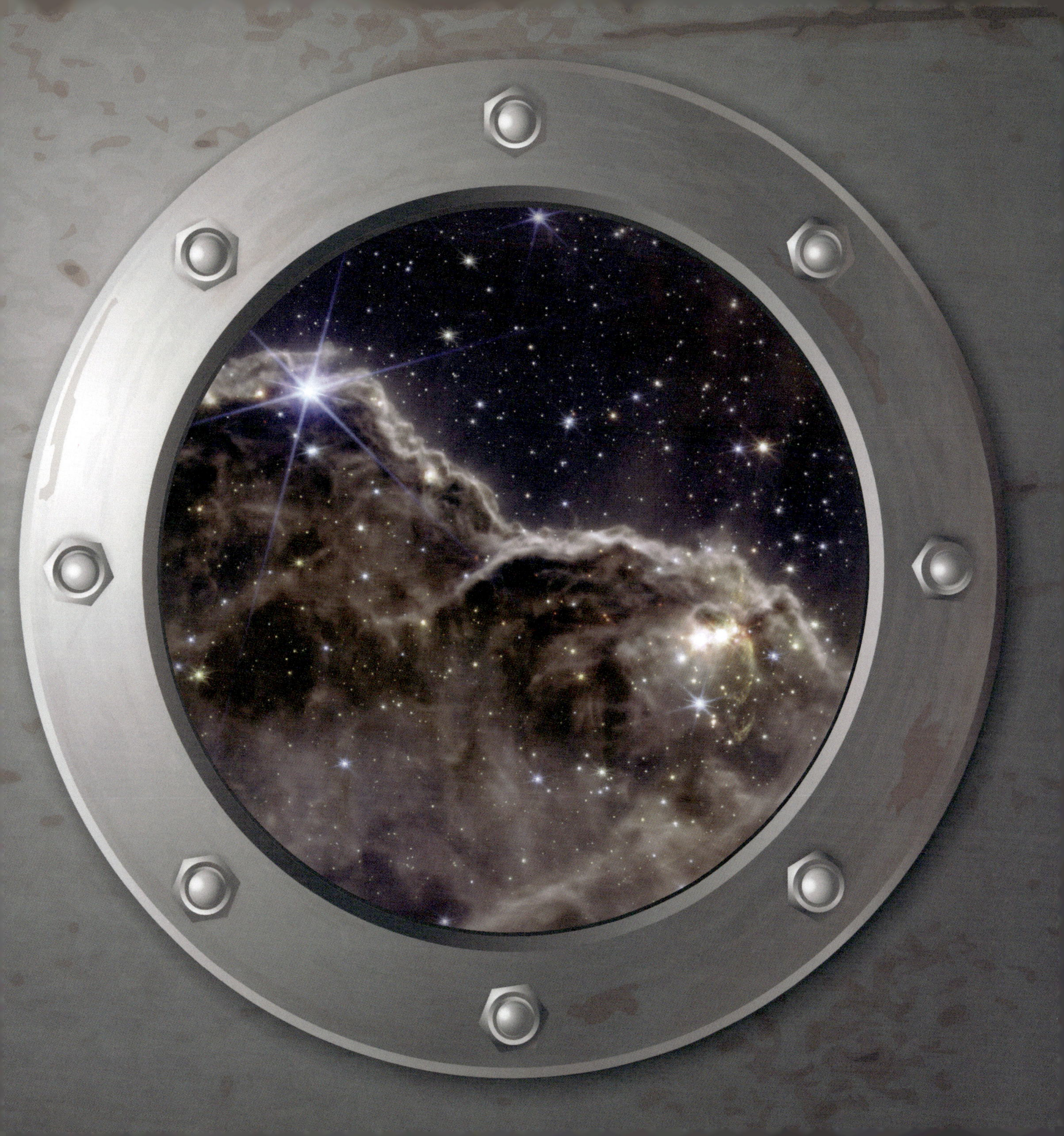

This is another picture of the Cosmic Cliffs, a part of the **Carina Nebula**. This nursery for stars is about 7,600 light years away from Earth.

Can you see the "steam" rising from the clouds? That's actually hot gas and dust!

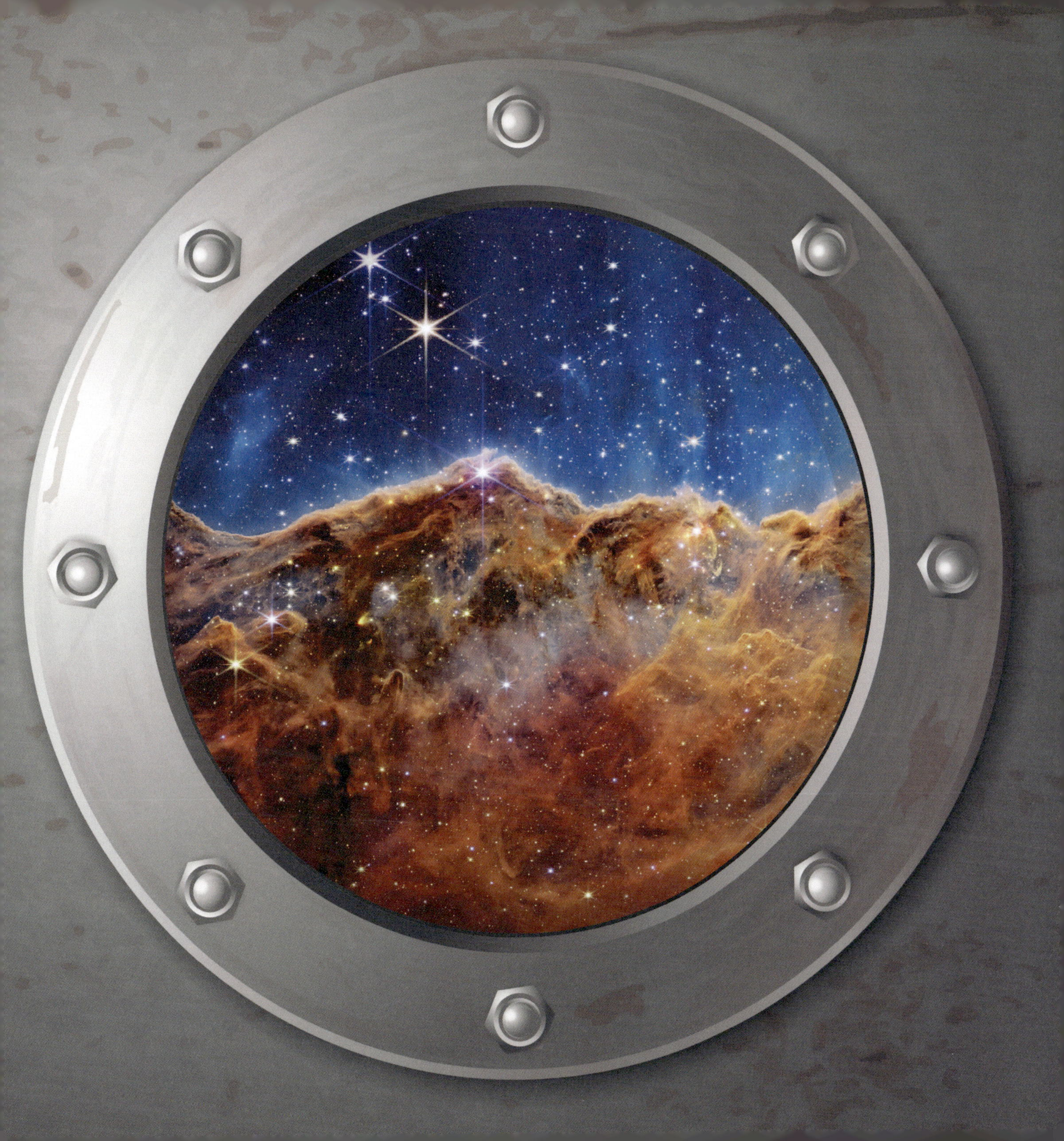

Galaxies are star systems made up of hundreds of billions of stars. This picture is of the **Cartwheel Galaxy** (named because it looks like a wheel on a cart).

The Cartwheel Galaxy is *500 million* light years away from Earth and, at 144,000 light years across, it is quite a bit larger than our own galaxy—the Milky Way.

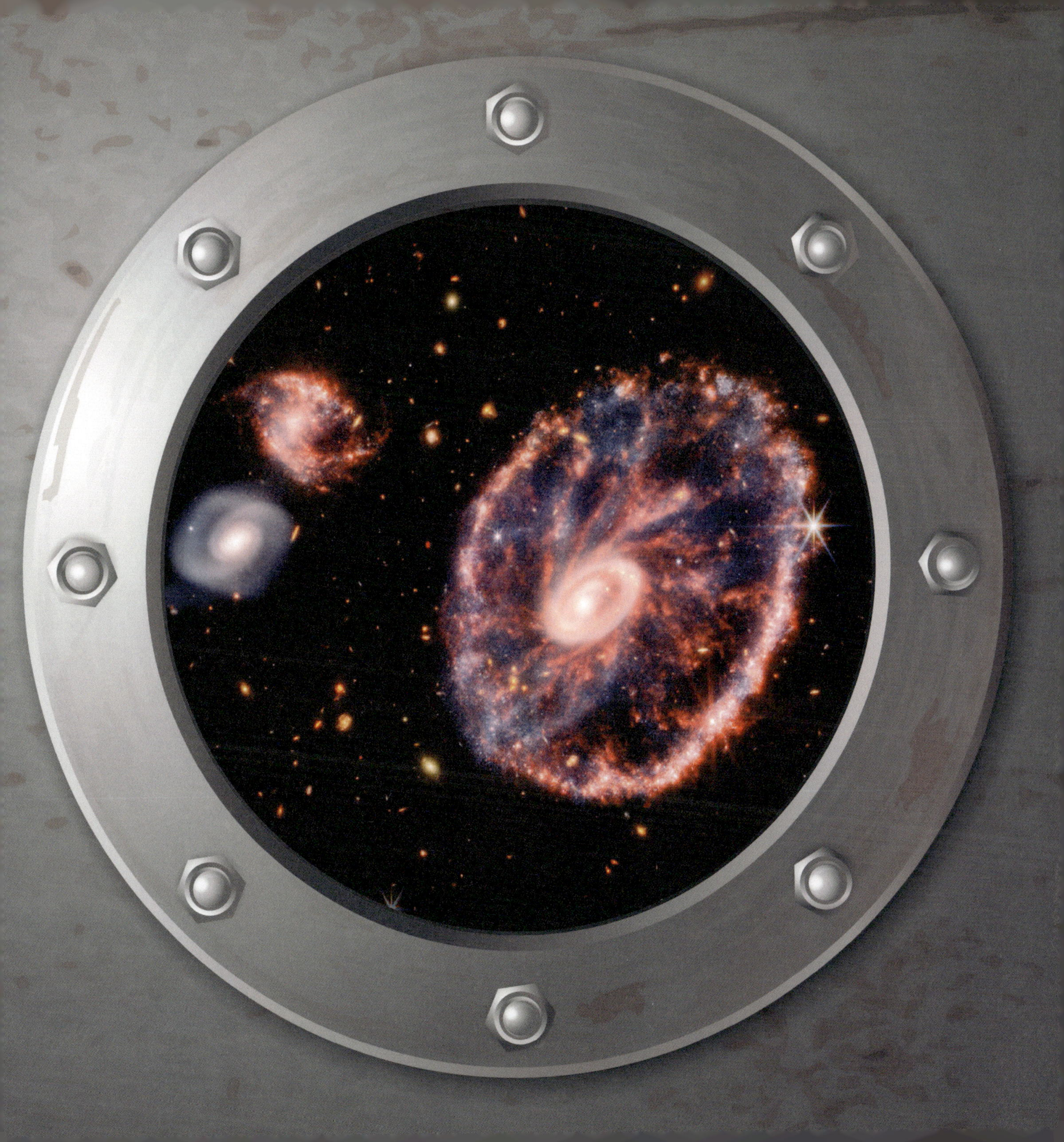

What's better than one galaxy? Try *five!* **Stephan's Quintet** is a collection of five different galaxies that are clustered together in what is called a compact group.

Can you find the two galaxies that are crashing into each other? *Someday, they will turn into one giant galaxy!*

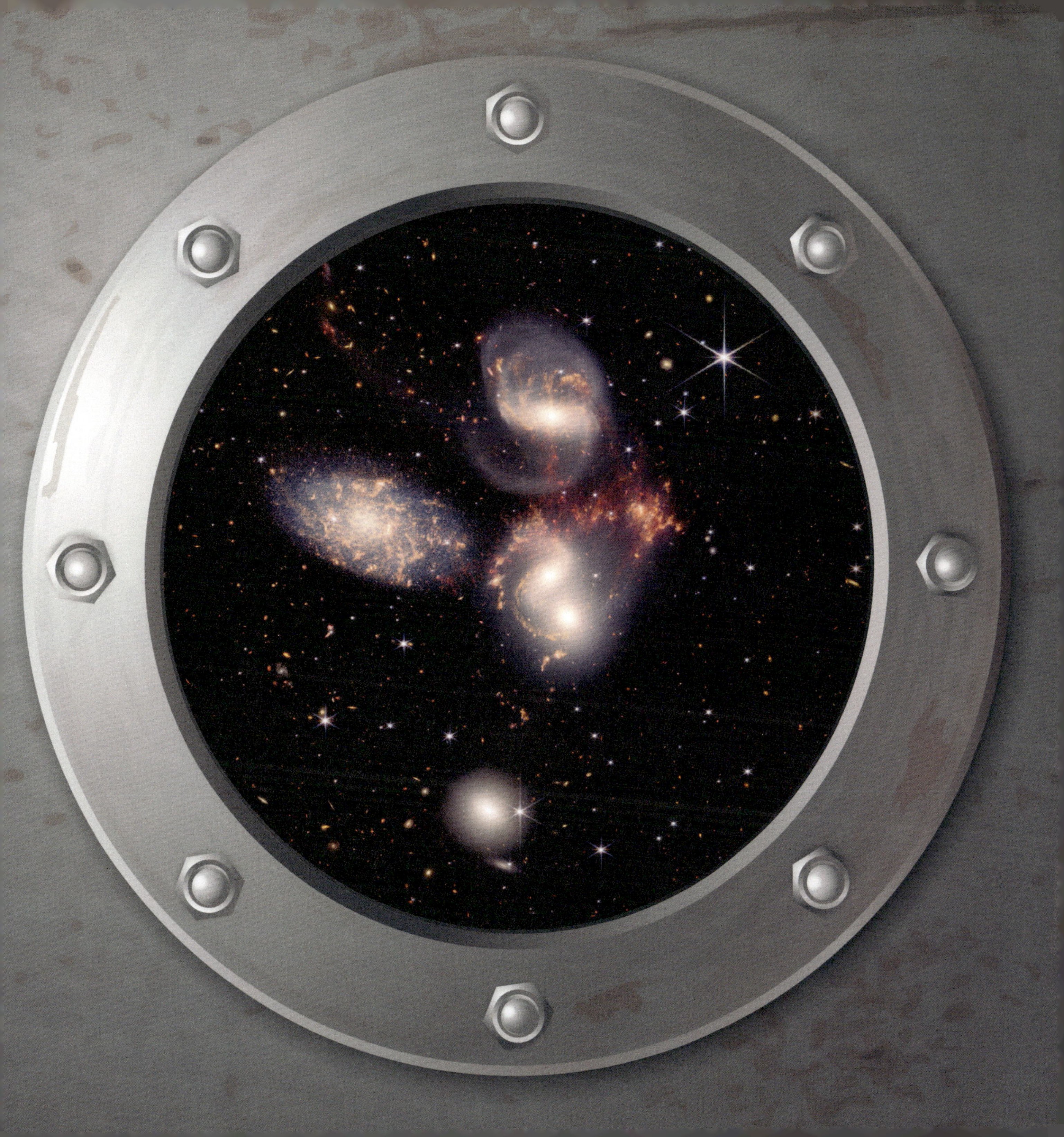

Alright, astronauts, let's end with a bang!

Those aren't stars you're seeing—those are thousands of *galaxies*.

We are looking so deep into the universe here that the tiniest galaxies in this picture are so old that they're forming just after the Big Bang. With the James Webb Space Telescope, we can see back to the birth of the universe.

Come on, let's get a better view.

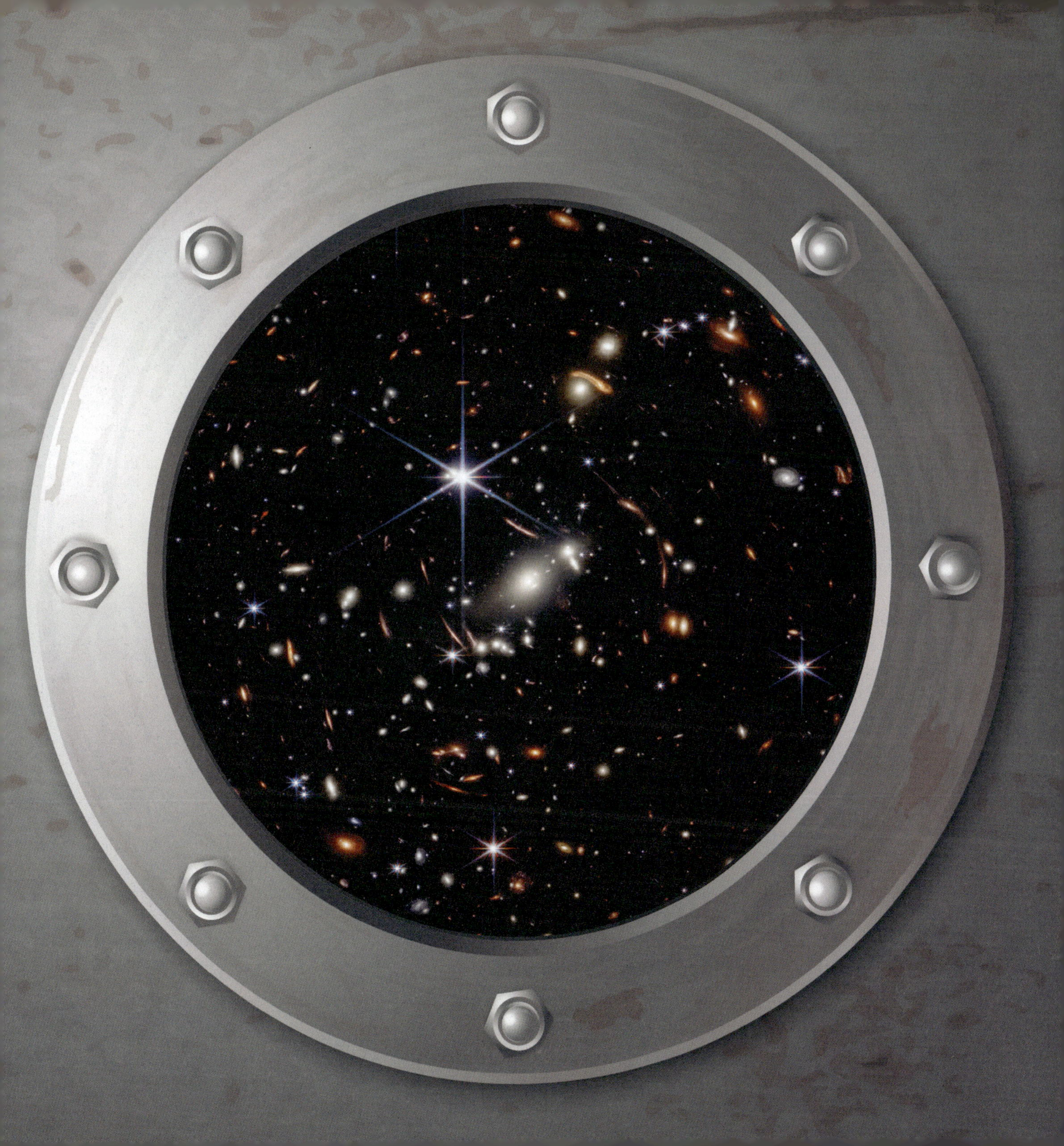

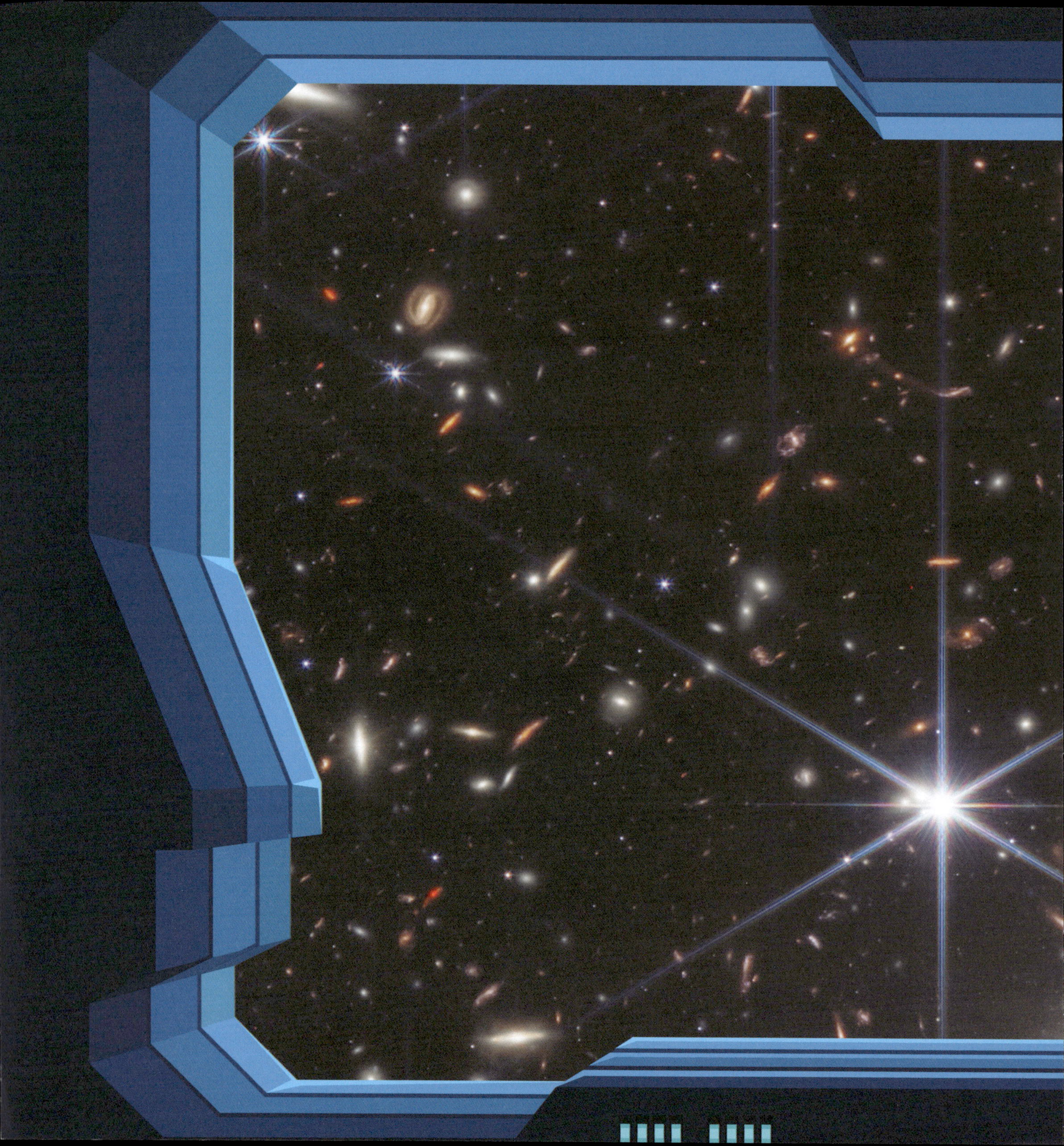

How cool is THAT?

SOLAR SYSTEM

SUN · MERCURY · VENUS · EARTH · MARS · JUPITER · SATURN · URANUS · NEPTUNE

Printed in Great Britain
by Amazon